ALAIN PROUST: PORTRAIT OF CAPE TOWN

At the foot of famed Table Mountain lies the Mother City and, by its rejuvenated harbour, the Victoria & Alfred Waterfront, in the heart of which stands the palatial new Table Bay hotel.

FERNWOOD PRESS
P O BOX 15344
VLAEBERG 8018

REGISTRATION NUMBER 90/04463/07

FIRST PUBLISHED 1994
SECOND EDITION 1998

COPYRIGHT © PHOTOGRAPHS ALAIN PROUST, 1998, EXCEPT FOR:
ANDREW INGPEN, PAGE 11 (BELOW); NIC BOTHMA, PAGE 82;
KEN FINDLAY, PAGES 83 (CENTRE), 90 (CENTRE).
COPYRIGHT © TEXT PETER BORCHERT, 1998
COPYRIGHT © SATELLITE PHOTOGRAPH ON PAGE 6 SATELLITE
APPLICATIONS CENTRE, MIKONTEC, CSIR, PRETORIA

DESIGN BY WILLEM JORDAAN, CAPE TOWN
EDITED BY LENI MARTIN AND SEAN FRASER, CAPE TOWN
PRODUCTION CONTROL BY ABDUL LATIEF (BUNNY) GALLIE, CAPE TOWN
TYPESETTING BY ALIX GRACIE, CAPE TOWN
REPRODUCTION BY UNIFOTO (PTY) LTD, CAPE TOWN
PRINTED AND BOUND BY TIEN WAH PRESS (PTE) LTD, SINGAPORE

ISBN 1 874950 38 5

# ALAIN PROUST PORTRAIT OF CAPE TOWN

## TEXT BY PETER BORCHERT

FERNWOOD
PRESS

*To my wife Mary, and our sons Nicolas and Jacques*

**P**ortrait of Cape Town *is a reflection of those aspects of the city and its surrounds that appeal to my aesthetic sense. I love the mountain and its environment, the crisp light of early morning and the warm light of evening. I love the contrasting seasons and the many moods of the sea and sky, and I am constantly inspired by the grandeur of the setting.*

*I hope that these images will show a vision of Cape Town that may be shared by Capetonians and visitors alike.* Portrait of Cape Town *is my own tribute to the extraordinary place that has become my physical and spiritual home.*

ALAIN PROUST CAPE TOWN 1998

ROBBEN ISLAND

TABLE BAY

CAPE TOWN

SEA POINT

CLIFTON

CAMPS BAY

LLANDUDNO

HOUT BAY

STRANDFONTEIN

MUIZENBERG

ST JAMES

NOORDHOEK

KALK BAY

FISH HOEK

KOMMETJIE

GLENCAIRN

SIMON'S TOWN

FALSE BAY

ATLANTIC OCEAN

SMITSWINKEL BAY

CAPE POINT

CAPE OF GOOD HOPE

This satellite photograph shows the Cape
Peninsula and part of the Cape Flats. The
dark, textured colouring represents mountain
areas; the dark red dense natural vegetation
shades to the lighter urban vegetation; the
light blue denotes urban development; and
the solid black areas are water bodies.

# The Cape Peninsula

N

0          KM          5

The soaring cliffs of Cape Point, for much of the year battered by high winds and crashing waves.

# INTRODUCTION

At the southern tip of the African continent a thin, gnarled finger of land projects defiantly into the Atlantic Ocean that all but surrounds it. Sculpted by time and the elements, this peninsula is a place of great beauty, dominated by an imposing mountainous spine that in places drops sheer into the sea and terminates, at its northern limit, in the Table Mountain massif. It is this mountain, with Lion's Head and Devil's Peak, that is the backdrop to Cape Town, Africa's most southerly city and the home of some four million people.

No-one knows for sure when man first came to the Cape, but it was undoubtedly a long time ago. Archaeological evidence suggests that the peninsula may have been settled as long as 100 000 years ago but, although other sites along the coast seem to corroborate these findings, the record is frustratingly incomplete.

At some stage between these early settlements and the arrival of Europeans, communities of yellow-skinned herders established themselves at the Cape and these were the indigenous

A rank of tall pines lines the road to the summit of Signal Hill.

people whom European explorers first encountered at the end of the fifteenth century. But time and the people of northern Europe were not kind to these small, gracile pastoralists and they were soon relegated to oblivion.

Although Arabian, Indian, Chinese or even Phoenician merchants may have been the first seamen to round Cape Point, the course of uninterrupted recorded history begins with the Portuguese mariners of the late 15th century who sailed into the unknown in search of an alternative trade route to the Orient. That they stepped ashore here is entrenched in history but they never laid claim to the land and it thus fell to the Dutch, highly successful competitors in the lucrative trade with the East, to establish a permanent settlement at the foot of Table Mountain.

For a century and a half, the will of Holland held sway at the Cape. The tiny settlement, with its wood-and-mud fort and meagre buildings, began to grow into a town of some size, with imposing edifices, wide dusty streets, noisome canals and an impressive five-bastioned castle complete with moat.

During this period, farms were established in what are now the suburbs of the city, vines were planted, and slaves imported from other parts of Africa and the East. It was these newcomers from the Dutch East India Company's far-flung colonial possessions – such as Java and elsewhere in Indonesia – who were the forebears of the people now known as the Cape Malays, a strongly cohesive Muslim community that has contributed hugely to Cape Town and its cosmopolitan character.

And then came the British. Their first arrival was tentative and short-lived, but in 1806 an expeditionary force landed at Blaauwberg and soon, following a short and decisive battle with the Dutch, the Union Jack fluttered from the seat of government – and continued to do so for the next 150 years. The British way became indelibly engraved on life and society at the Cape; industry and commerce grew in stature and with it an emergent Cape Town began to spread its wings. The imposing Victorian and Edwardian style of the Empire began to raise their turrets, domes and spires above the skyline, jostling with the sterner, plainer lines of Dutch architecture. The harbour grew in tandem with the British merchant fleet, and Cape Town basked in a maritime importance to match other far-flung ports of the colonies.

But the tentacles of imperialism were not always greeted with enthusiasm by those already occupying the land. Bitter border struggles were fought with indigenous people to the east and in the north – where long-disgruntled Dutch-speaking pioneer farmers had trekked to establish their own promised land – antipathy towards the Cape government erupted into hostility and war, spurred on by the discovery of gold and diamonds.

Cape Town remained largely aloof and untouched by the bitter border struggles fought with indigenous people to the east and disgruntled Dutch-speaking pioneer farmers in the north. The city, aside from the bawdy, rough life of the harbour taverns and the rude dwellings of its less prosperous inhabitants, was a place of high society, with banquets and balls in the homes of note, horse racing on the common and elegant carriage rides down oak- and plane-lined avenues.

The Cape was also moving slowly towards independent government, and the foundation of an economic infrastructure was being laid, while hospitals, schools and other seats of higher learning were being established. Cape Town, too, became a focus of the scientific world. Dilettante botanists and natural historians came to collect specimens and to wonder over the evolutionary miracle of the Cape flora.

Such intrigue with the natural world was typical of this age of enquiry and enlightenment. At the Cape, however, it found added expression, for here on this tiny peninsula at the end of the world more than 2 600 species of plants have been identified and Table Mountain itself has more than 1 400 indigenous species – little wonder that it is a national monument, the focus of a new national park, and awaiting declaration as a World Heritage Site.

It is not for aesthetic reasons alone that the mountain chain of the peninsula is treasured, however; there are sound social and economic reasons as well. Table Mountain is undoubtedly one of the most recognised landmarks of the world and has huge recreational and ecotourism value. If wisely managed, it has the potential to earn substantial revenue for Cape Town.

It is sadly ironic, then, that this extraordinarily beautiful tip to the African continent, blessed with so much, has also been the setting for so much human suffering. The entire country has witnessed and felt the crushing might of colonial powers and, more recently, the well documented flaunting of human rights during the apartheid years. But the spirit of Cape Town and its people remain indomitable as they continue to tackle the problems that derive from being one of the world's fastest-growing conurbations.

In world terms, Cape Town is a young city, a mere three and half centuries into its life, but it is the oldest city in southern Africa and, as such, is steeped in the history of the land and its people. At almost every turn there is something – a cobbled street, some Victorian ironwork, a Cape Dutch façade, or a stately old tree – to remind one of a bygone era. But it is also a modern city, filled with vibrancy, enthusiasm and confidence.

Cape Town seems to have everything: mountains, forests, beautiful beaches, winelands and some of the finest architecture in the land. But it has more than just physical beauty; it has a soul.

Tucked between the cityscape and the ocean, lie the docklands of Table Bay.

*T*he northern face of Table Mountain, with Devil's Peak at its eastern buttress, rises a thousand meters above central Cape Town while, not as imposing, Lion's Head – sloping down to Signal Hill – flanks the city to the west. Southwards, the rugged spine of the Table Mountain chain extends virtually without interruption to Cape Point. Thwarted only by the sea and the famed mountain, Capetonians have woven a close fabric of buildings that overlies every available square inch of real estate. In one instance, not even the ocean has succeeded as a barrier, for the natural contour of Table Bay has been somewhat altered by the development of Duncan Dock as Cape Town's main harbour. In the process of its construction, started in 1938, some 194 hectares were reclaimed from the sea, giving the city its Foreshore which has never been successfully integrated with the Mother City. To the west and south, Cape Town manages to squeeze past the headland of Signal Hill, continuing in a ribbon of development along the Atlantic coast. To the north and east, however, it escapes via a wider passage between land and sea. This is where the sprawl of greater Cape Town begins – like the floodwaters of a storm, people and their dwellings spread out over the flat, sandy isthmus that joins Cape Town to its hinterland.

The city and mountain loom behind vessels in the harbour (left) and the V&A Waterfront development (below).

Paint is stripped from the hull of a Taiwanese trawler.

*T*able Mountain dominates the city from almost every angle, dwarfing the small central business district with its skyline of moderately high-rise office towers. The area between the docklands and the city is rapidly being remodelled to link it to the main Waterfront developments (off to the right of the photograph above) skirting Table Bay. Although there is a bustle and a sense of purpose in Cape Town's harbour environs the likes of which has not been seen since the mid-1960s when hostilities in the Middle East led to the closure of the Suez Canal, the port works well below its capacity. In fact, never in recent times has Cape Town been South Africa's busiest harbour – that status belongs to Durban which alone accounts for some 50 per cent of the country's sea freight.

*For more than 20 years, Cape Town was effectively separated from its water-front by the Foreshore reclamation which placed hundreds of thousands of tonnes of landfill between the city and its harbour – a sad and ironic fate for a port long known throughout the maritime world as the Tavern of the Seas. Happily, all bad things come to an end and, in the early 1990s, a bold scheme took shape, inspired by other contemporary dockland redevelopments as far afield as Sydney, London and Los Angeles. Around the old harbour – the Alfred Basin where sailing ships once moored and the adjacent Victoria Dock – old sheds,*

Previously separated from the hub of activity on the V&A Waterfront, the restaurant and Old Clock Tower on Bertie's Landing (opposite top) have now been linked to the Pier Head by a new swing bridge.

*warehouses and harbour buildings of historical and architectural note were carefully stripped and then refashioned with sensitivity and imagination. New buildings have been added, all skilfully designed to compliment the elegance and style of the past. Although not yet a decade old, the renascent V&A Waterfront has refocused Cape Town's leisure and entertainment attention, becoming in the process one of the places to shop, eat and have fun. Several hotels offering a degree of luxury to compare with the best, provide visitors with the opportunity of staying in one of the most spectacular waterfront environments in the world.*

*T*he retail hub of the V&A Waterfront is the huge Victoria Wharf shopping complex – virtually a city within a city, where supermarkets, bookstores and cinemas rub shoulders with clothing boutiques, African art and curio galleries, and other speciality shops and stalls. Eating (and drinking), however, is the major activity at the Waterfront, with restaurants and pubs catering to all tastes and pockets from haute cuisine and ethnic through to steakhouses, coffee shops, ice-cream parlours and open-air food stalls. Busking and street theatre add to the Waterfront's ongoing carnival atmosphere, as do the rhythms of jazz escaping through the windows and doors of restaurants such as the Green Dolphin on a hot summer's night. Just as likely, however, it will be an orchestra playing Mozart or the compelling percussion of an African marimba band that courts the ear. Cosmopolitan the Waterfront certainly is, and made even more so by the presence of international brands such as the Hard Rock Café and Planet Hollywood. Powerful as these modern icons of western life are, however, the Waterfront's identity as a place uniquely Cape Town is unchallenged.

From the lofty Victoria Wharf shopping mall (opposite top) to the lively bustle of the Hard Rock Café (opposite below) and the new Planet Hollywood (above), the V&A is well entrenched as one of Cape Town's leading attractions.

The kelp tank, one the major displays at the Two Oceans Aquarium.

Diners enjoy the ambience of a restaurant within the working harbour of the Victoria Basin.

*The V&A Waterfront development lies primarily along the eastern flank of the Alfred and Victoria basins. Although the piers and quays have been given over to entertainment, the old harbour still works for its living, with fishing and other craft constantly on the move. The principal commercial life of Cape Town's harbour, however, lies to the west in the Duncan Dock, which was opened in 1943, and in the huge container and bulk handling terminal. Once the graceful mailships of the Union-Castle Line and other shipping companies were regular visitors to the Duncan Dock but, apart from a few visiting pleasure cruisers, the days of the passenger liners are sadly past. For the most part, the main harbour is a bleak and uninviting place with none of the charm of the Waterfront where among the main attractions is the world-class Two Oceans Aquarium. The name derives from the two oceans – the Atlantic and the Indian – that sweep the South African coast. Although it does have displays of highly coloured coral reef fishes, the aquarium's focus is on the marine habitats and species that characterise the colder water environment of the southern and western Cape coasts.*

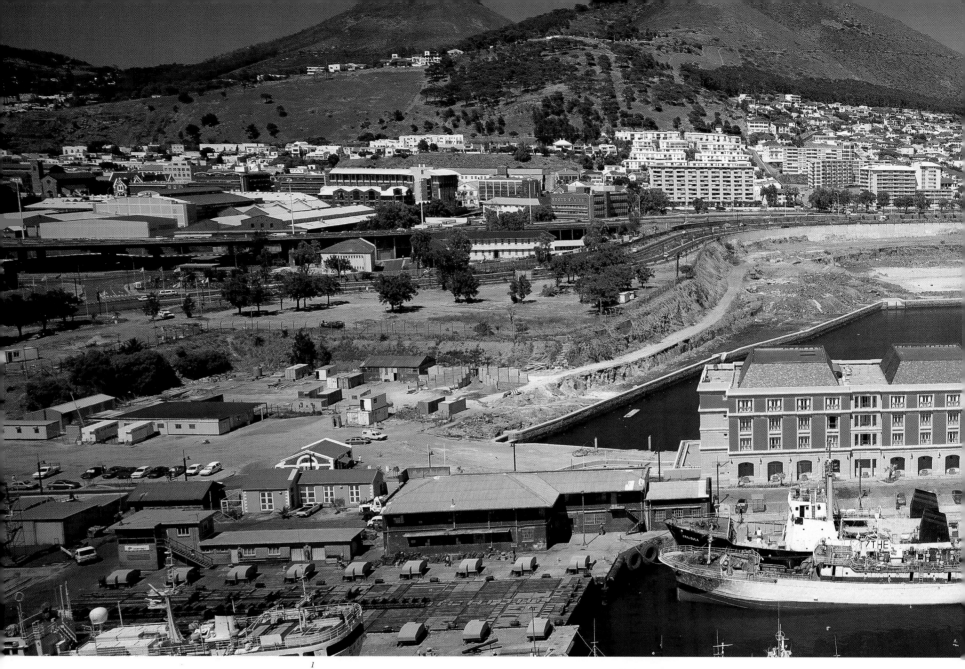

1
2

*A*lthough Cape Town has always been popular with travellers, it is only in the last few years that tourism to the city has burgeoned to the extent that, at times, it has been nigh on impossible to secure accommodation unless booked well in advance. This sustained demand has spawned a host of new establishments, from modest bed-and-breakfast hostelries – many of them with their origins in rapidly converted suburban homes – to the recently completed Cape Grace and The Table Bay hotels on the Waterfront.

As Cape Town enjoys an unprecedented boom in the hospitality industry, these new luxury hotels – boasting impeccable service, plush accommodation and enviable views across the expanse of Table Bay – are rapidly emerging to take their place as the city base for visiting dignitaries and celebrities.

Still standing proudly in the face of competition from its more modern counterparts are the gracious old Mount Nelson Hotel in the heart of the city and, also noted for its understated elegance, The Vineyard Hotel in Newlands.

1 Cape Grace Hotel, V&A Waterfront.
2 Gardens of The Vineyard Hotel, Newlands.
3 The Table Bay, V&A Waterfront.
4 The Bay Hotel, Camps Bay.
5 Mount Nelson Hotel, Gardens.

3
4
5

1 Robben Island, with the city in the distance.
2 Visitors are ferried to the island.
3 The Governor's House, a base for visiting dignitaries.
4 The island's coastline is littered with wrecks.
5 Anglican church, built for the lepers in 1841.

5

*Robben Island lies just beyond the immediate confines of Table Bay, about 10 kilometres across from the Mouille Point lighthouse. It is low, windswept and forbidding, made even more so by its long association with human misery and hardship. Almost continuously, from the time that western man set foot on its shores to exploit seals, its seabirds for their eggs, and its stone for building, the island has served as a penal settlement, leper colony, lunatic asylum and prison. More recently, its notoriety has centred around the fact that South Africa's president, Nelson Mandela, and many of his colleagues were held on the island for so long as political prisoners. Today Robben Island is a National Monument and* the South African government has applied for it to be declared a World Heritage Site. A central development has been the establishment of the Robben Island Museum, designed to embrace the educational, ecological, tourism and conservation aspects of the island. The museum also includes the Mayibuye Centre, originally housed at the University of the Western Cape, which holds an extraordinary collection of files, documents, photographs and other artifacts recording the lives and times of those who actively opposed apartheid. A pilgrimage to the island is high on the agenda for most visitors to Cape Town, the crossing now reduced to a mere 20 minutes on a fast, twin-hulled ferry.*

1

2

1  Harbour and Foreshore.
2  Courtyard, Martin Melck House.
3 & 4  Heritage Square, Bree Street.
5  The noon-day gun, Signal Hill.

3

4

*T*he top of Signal Hill, from where the noon-day gun still sends its watch-setting boom across the harbour and inner city, provides one of the finest vantage points for viewing the full sweep of Table Bay. Directly below lies the city bowl, incorporating both the business district and gracious reminders of the old colonial settlement, most notable in the charm of Heritage Square on Bree Street. Between the modern city and the waters of Table Bay lies the Waterfront, with the Duncan Dock and container terminal off to the right. Beyond, the bay curves gently to the north, fringed along its shore first by the light industrial area of Paardeneiland and then by the successive suburbs of Milnerton, Table View, Blouberg and Melkbosstrand.

*C*ape Town's flea-market culture extends far beyond the Grand Parade, its original venue, and these days stallholders gather gypsy-like at various sites throughout the Peninsula. Almost every suburb has its own regular Saturday or Sunday market and the range of goods on offer is prodigious: leatherware, handmade clothes, pottery, antique bottles, stamps, brassware, general bric-a-brac. The most famous of the flea markets is probably that held daily on Greenmarket Square in the city itself. The leafy square, with its cobbled streets and perimeter of handsome buildings – including the Old Town House with its baroque façade, an Art Deco

hotel and the Gothic-style Metropolitan Mthodist Church – is a gathering place for locals and visitors alike. The market is an enthusiastic crush of tightly packed stalls and brightly coloured umbrellas. And always there is music to add to the general hubbub: marimba, jazz and the classics. Capetonians have always enjoyed their small speciality shops and the markets with their general informality. In the not so distant past, expressions of spontaneity such as those shown on Greenmarket Square were frowned on by the city fathers, but now the casual bustle is an accepted part of Cape Town's personality.

1 Exhibiting artists, St George's Mall.
2 Long Street.
3 City reflections.
4 The mountain peeps from behind modern high-rises.
5 Looking down on St George's Mall.

4

5

*While some of Cape Town's high-rise buildings may have individual merit, most are simply functional with little to set them apart from those that crowd the central business district of any modern city. Only glimpses of the mountain behind place them without doubt. The grace and charm of the Mother City come mostly from bygone, colonial times and from the Capetonians who live and work here today. In a largely successful attempt to enhance the appearance of the inner city, St George's Street which runs parallel to Adderley Street, Cape Town's main thoroughfare, has been relieved of its choking traffic to become a leafy pedestrian mall, peopled by a constant parade of locals and visitors. At the head of the street, the roof of St George's Cathedral is just visible. The cathedral is the seat of the Archbishop of Cape Town, head of the Anglican Church in South Africa. Many worthy clerics have borne this title, but none has won the hearts and minds of so many, not only of South Africans but of the world at large, than the now retired but still indefatigable Desmond Tutu.*

1  Buildings old and new on Long Street.
2  Down Long Street towards the harbour.
3  Eclectic collectibles of a Long Street shop.
4  Mama Africa offers a unique African menu.
5  Shop fronts line the old-world thoroughfare.
6  Interiors decorated with images of Africa.
7  The trendy new Long Street Café.

3

4  5

*L*ong Street must be the most photographed thoroughfare of the city, for more than any other it manifests the extraordinary amalgamation of cultures that have made Cape Town. At its lower end, where it joins the Foreshore, its character has been destroyed by irresponsible development, but as it journeys uphill towards the mountain it comes alive with churches, mosques, shops and hostelries representing and combining the whole gamut of period and style that has dictated Cape Town's architectural heritage. Overall, however, it is Victorian in character, with Art Nouveau and Art Deco detail and with cast-iron railings and 'broekie lace' decorating the balconies and verandahs. Among the most notable buildings are the Blue Lodge, originally a rooming house and now Cape Town's only remaining example of a High Victorian corner building; the Palm Tree Mosque; the Green Hansom Hotel; the YMCA; and undoubtedly one of Cape Towns loveliest architectural memorials, the Sendinggestig (Mission Foundation).

6

7

The Standard Bank, Adderley Street.

City Hall, Darling Street. Lower Burg Street.

Lower Burg Street.

*I*n many of the city's central streets, contemporary office blocks crowd tightly together as they compete for the sky, but here and there a grand old lady presides, pushing pretenders to the side and creating both light and space. In Adderley Street, the Standard Bank building first rose above the city in 1880. It was heightened during the 1920s, but the central dome with its figure of Britannia remained to remind the city of Victoria and the Empire. The façade of the bank is graced by a classical portico of impressive proportion that stands a full two storeys above the street. Inside, the architecture of the banking hall has been compromised by the demands of a modern financial institution, but the rich mahogany tellers' booths and the lofty columns bearing an ornate ceiling remain. Around the corner, in Darling Street, is the City Hall, a majestic building in the Italian Renaissance style. It is of later vintage than the Standard Bank, the foundation stone having been laid only in 1900 and the building completed in 1905. Ironically, the city had no civic focus until this time, although the suburbs already had long-established municipalities, each with its own town hall. The administration of Cape Town has moved to a soulless slab on the Foreshore but City Hall remains the symbol of civic authority. Hopefully, when the current refurbishments are complete, the grand hall with its magnificent Norman Beard organ, will again be home to the Cape Town Philharmonic Orchestra.

Entrance to the South African Museum.

Elaborate ironwork – whether purely decorative or also functional – is a hallmark of the Victorian period.

*I*t has been said that the South African Museum, with its peculiarly Republican style, could well have stood on Church Square in Pretoria instead of at the top end of the Gardens above Parliament in Cape Town. Not surprisingly, perhaps, for the man who designed it in 1893 happened to be the government architect of the Boer Republic of the Orange Free State. The interior of the building has been much altered over the years, although the majestic main staircase remains. Among the museums many attractions is the Whale Room where the full skeleton of a blue whale hangs in the vault-like chamber, seeming to glide peacefully through the subdued light. The Whale Room, renowned for its acoustics, is the venue of many music recitals. A San display in another part of the museum depicts aspects of the culture of these early inhabitants of southern Africa, including their world-famous rock art. Adjacent to the museum, in Queen Victoria Street, is the Planetarium, where popular lectures and courses on the wonders of the southern skies are told.

1

2

3

4

1 Main Road, Woodstock.
2 Schotsche Kloof.
3 Mosque, Long Street.
4 Lutheran Church, Strand Street.
5 Buitenkant Street.
6 Colonial verandah, Tuynhuis.
7 Strand Street.
8 Old Somerset Hospital.

5

6

7

*I*f one were to wander around Cape Town with an enquiring mind and inquisitive eye, the buildings of the city would tell of its history far more eloquently than any textbook could. For the architecture of Cape Town and its surrounds is interwoven with the history of the people who have lived here, from the founding settlement of the Dutch through to the present. During the period of Dutch tenure, which lasted more or less from 1652 until the close of the 1700s, French and other Europeans settled at the Cape. In fact, for a time they were actively encouraged to do so by Dutch authorities keen to bolster their fledgling colony against the possibility of British domination. Artisans were especially welcome. The Muslim community, too, was established during this time and many of these immigrants from the East were also artisans. At the zenith of the Dutch East India Company, fine buildings came to grace the growing city, many owing their design and detail to the genius of Louis Michel Thibault, a Frenchman, and the German sculptor, Anton Anreith. But, by the early nineteenth century, the British were here to stay and the style of architecture changed completely: Regency, Georgian, Victorian and Edwardian.

Jan Hendrik ('Onze Jan') Hofmeyr, scholar and politician.

Jan Smuts.

Queen Victoria.

Cecil John Rhodes

Sir George Grey.

War Memorial, Gardens.

General Louis Botha.

Bartholomeu Dias.

*I*t is said that the writing of history is the prerogative of the victor, and certainly the statuary of Cape Town lends credence to this view, for the city abounds with the bronze and stone images of past notables. Bartholomeu Dias and Jan van Riebeeck are there, as are Jan Smuts and Louis Botha who, although both defeated Boer generals, regained their status and more as early prime ministers of the Union of South Africa. Queen Victoria, too, is there still gazing out over one of the many dominions she ruled but never saw. One of her greatest champions was Cecil John Rhodes, arch imperialist, business tycoon and politician. He was a man of huge ambition and vision who dreamt of an Anglo-Africa reaching from Cape to Cairo. His influence, whether for good or bad, on the affairs of southern Africa was immense, but in 1902 he died dishonoured after an abortive attempt to seize control of the Transvaal Republic.

Luthern Church, Strand Street.

*T*he Lutheran Church, with its Gothic and classical detailing, owes its existence to Martin Melck, a prosperous farmer of the late eighteenth century and a leader in the small but growing Lutheran community. In 1771, Melck gave his fellow worshippers permission to hold services in his barn on Strand Street. A few years later, with the advent of greater religious tolerance, the barn was converted into a church, its façade designed by Anton Anreith, one of the country's most renowned architects. To the east of the church, Melck set aside land for a parsonage which was completed after his death. Known as Martin Melck House, it was also designed by Anreith and is regarded as a particularly fine example of a townhouse of the period.

Bree Street

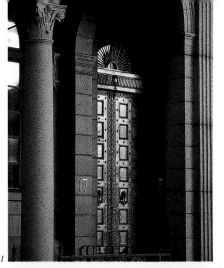

1  Cultural History Museum, Church Square.
2  Corporation Street.
3  Waterkant Street.
4  Adderley Street.

*K*oopmans-De Wet House has a history reaching back to the early eighteenth century. It subsequently passed through many hands and many alterations, gaining its present façade and proportions at the hands of the redoubtable team of Thibault and Anreith. In the early 1800s, the house was bought by the De Wet family, in whose hands it remained until 1911. In the latter part of the nineteenth century it was occupied by Maria, a daughter who had married Johan Koopmans in 1864.

When Maria was widowed, she and her sister continued to live at the Strand Street residence, directing their considerable energies into assembling a fine collection of period furniture. Today Koopmans-De Wet House is a museum and well worth a visit, for it is redolent of the past century when it became a crossroads for the rich and famous of the time – dignitaries such as Cecil John Rhodes and Paul Kruger were among those graciously received by the hospitable De Wet sisters.

*F*ew people, Capetonians included, have any idea of what lies beyond the guarded entrance to the Tuynhuis at the bottom of Roeland Street. Certainly there is no hint of the beautifully laid out formal gardens to the rear of the building that now houses the State President's Office. The security is understandable, but it is a pity that so few people may see this magnificent structure, which was built at the end of the seventeenth century as the guest house of the Dutch East India Company. Next door, the Houses of Parliament are of a much later vintage, for they were officially opened only in 1884. Later, at the time of Union, a new wing was brought into use to accommodate the House of Assembly. The Houses of Parliament have witnessed the full gamut of South Africa's modern history, including changes that for a time seemed impossible: transition from the deliberate creation of a land divided on the basis of skin colour to the recent process of healing. The imposing pile of Victorian and Edwardian opulence, once a symbol of prejudice and intolerance, now presides as a symbol of hope for the future of the country. One of the oldest structures in Cape Town is 'The Castle', or more correctly, The Castle of Good Hope. The cornerstone was laid in 1666 and for the next 13 years timber was dragged from Hout Bay, stone was shipped from Robben Island quarries and lime from shells was burnt on the beaches to construct what has been a symbol of military authority ever since. Over the centuries it has been added to and altered, but the original five-bastioned design remains.

1 Front courtyard, Castle of Good Hope.
2 Formal Gardens, Tuynhuis.
3 Simon van der Stel Gateway, Castle of Good Hope.
4 Kat Balcony, Castle of Good Hope.
5 Castle of Good Hope.
6 Houses of Parliament on Government Avenue.
7 Changing of the Guard, Castle of Good Hope

The ubiquitous grey
squirrel – an engaging
immigrant from Europe.

*T*he area around the Houses of Parliament and other
stately buildings that grace the city at the top of Adderley
Street is known simply as the Gardens. Bisected by Government
Avenue – flanked and canopied by venerable oaks – the Gardens
are a little corner of tranquillity, a much-needed green lung for
the city. They are a place to stroll, or to sit and have lunch, a place
to feed squirrels or simply to watch the world go by. Although
steeped in history, the Gardens are very much part of Cape Town
today and it is, perhaps, a little difficult to imagine them in the
role for which they were originally intended.

The upper balcony of Tuynhuis.

The raison d'être *for the early Dutch settlement was as a replenishment station for the merchantmen of the Dutch East India Company. It was with some urgency, therefore, that planting began, but the soils and the Cape climate were not kind and first attempts at cultivation met with little success. But in time, and under the supervision of the appropriately named Hendrik Boom, the Company Gardens began to take shape. For a while, they served their purpose, but soon agriculture took on the guise of free enterprise as favoured company servants, Hendrik Boom among them, were released from their company contracts to begin farming for themselves. With this process, the focus of the original Gardens progressed from market garden to a collection of botanical specimens and, finally, to a place of recreation for the growing city.*

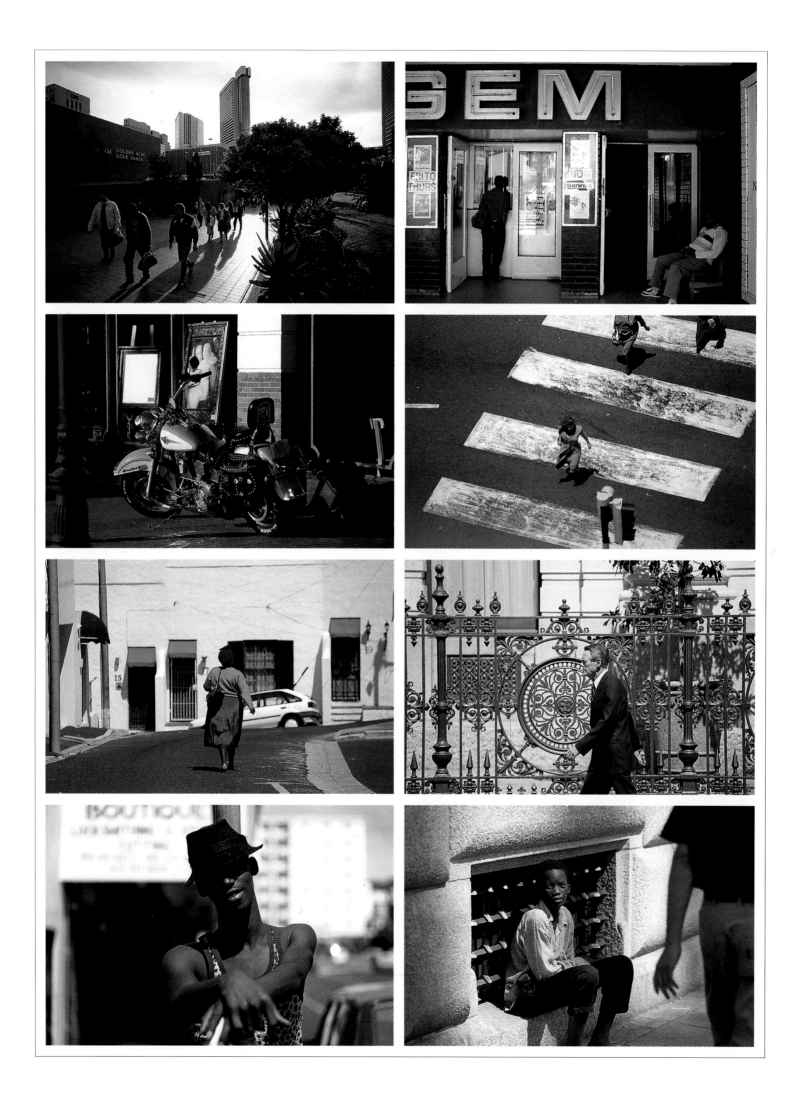

Longmarket Street.

St George's Street Mall.

*There was a time when Cape Town was a far more 'lived in' city, especially in the days before District Six was demolished and its people summarily moved out at the instruction of the architects of apartheid. Overcrowded and a slum District Six might have been, but it was a vibrant, colourful and integral part of Cape Town, which has been much the poorer for its passing. In recent decades, people have been drawn out of the city by the strong movement of business to the suburbs. Of course, people are still very much part of the city, but mostly as commuters moving daily to and from their places of work by car, bus, taxi and train. Planners are earnestly trying to win back popularity for the city centre, however, and with considerable success, particularly where streets have been closed to motor traffic and transformed into attractive pedestrian malls. Also, historic inner-city residential areas, such as around Loader Street (opposite, third row, left), are being rediscovered and restored in period style. Inner-city loft apartments, too, are becoming highly fashionable. Happily, the tide is thus turning and Capetonians are coming back into their city.*

*A*lthough Cape Town's suburbs are no longer pierced by the braying tones of the fish horn announcing the presence of an itinerant fishmonger, food from the sea is still sold throughout the Peninsula from carts, the backs of 'bakkies' (open vans) and street corners, especially when the much-prized snoek are running. In fact, there is not much that you cannot buy off the street in Cape Town, where the trade of hawking is as old as the city itself. Today, the so-called informal sector represents a substantial proportion of the local economy and provides a livelihood for thousands of Capetonians. Without it not only would they be materially worse off, but the city would be the poorer too. Cape Town would simply not be Cape Town without such long-established marketplaces as the Grand Parade where a deal can always be struck, whether over a bunch of dried traditional 'muti' herbs (bottom left), a bolt of brightly coloured fabric, a box of grapes, or a gold watch. The lively and often humorous banter between bargain-offering trader and sceptical customer, although all but incomprehensible to non-Capetonians, is an entertainment in itself.

Night falls over the city as workers make their way home in minibus taxis.

*During the height of summer, the sun sinks behind the mountains with apparent reluctance, leaving a lingering twilight to lengthen the evenings. But in winter it drops with almost indecent haste and city workers unable to make a quick getaway are likely to be finding their way home in the dark. For many, especially those who live far out in the townships and shanty towns that sprawl across the Cape Flats, the ride home will be in one of the minibus taxis lined up here as if for the start of Le Mans. As it happens, the analogy is not far from reality, for the taxi drivers are fiercely competitive and no quarter is given either to their colleagues on the road or to other motorists. The objective is to pack as many people as possible into their vehicles and to deliver them to their destination at the highest speed the straining motors can muster. Accidents do happen, but considering the velocity of these projectiles and the cavalier disregard for the highway code, it is a matter of some wonder that there are not more.*

Carnival time at New Year.

*N*ew Year is a special time in Cape Town: not only is it the height of the holiday season when beaches seethe with bodies and applause spatters out over the grandstands of Newlands Cricket Ground, but it is also the time of the Coon Carnival. The carnival, which centres around a number of Mardi Gras-style rallies and processions, was originally a celebration of the New Year among the Cape's slave community, but after slavery was abolished in the early nineteenth century the tradition lived on and grew to be an exuberant and highly colourful street spectacle, much enjoyed by the participants as well as the crowds that lined the routes to watch. After months of preparation, troupes of banjo- and guitar-playing minstrels in their boaters and bright silks would come pouring out of District Six and elsewhere – until the 1970s when, destructive officialdom reigning supreme, they were told that this would no longer be allowed. Today the carnival is largely confined to a few stadiums, but hopefully its cheerful sounds will soon ring once more through the city streets at New Year.

Flower sellers off Adderley Street.

*Another quintessential aspect of Cape Town life is the tradition of the flower seller. It would be hard to imagine a Cape Town without this doughty breed of women and men who are all but impossible to ignore when they decide, with all good humour, that you will buy their carnations, roses, glads...*

Great Synagogue, Gardens.

Mosque, Dorp Street.

Groote Kerk, Adderley Street.

*R*eligion being so often a divisive element in the world, it is perhaps surprising that in a country where social and political history has dwelt on the differences between people, the expression of worship has never led to the terrible conflicts experienced in other parts of the world. There are fundamental differences, of course, but by and large tolerance prevails and Christianity, Judaism and Islam, three of the world's greatest faiths, have played a huge role in the shaping of Cape Town. Churches, synagogues and mosques abound, many of them beautiful and fitting tributes not only to the Almighty, but also to the architectural genius of those who built them. Adding to the pervading calm of the Gardens is the Great Synagogue, its elegant baroque-style twin towers rising majestically above the trees. The synagogue was consecrated in 1905, but it was not the first place of worship for the colony's Jewry, for alongside is the Old Synagogue which was built in the Egyptian style in 1863 and is now the Jewish Museum. Not far from the Great Synagogue, at the city end of the Gardens, is the Groote Kerk. The church, built by Herman Schutte is a somewhat strange marriage of Gothic, Egyptian and classical elements. It was dedicated in 1841, but the adjacent baroque clock tower, the only remaining part of the original church building on the site, dates from the beginning of the 1700s.

Lutheran Church and mosque, Loop Street.

Moravian Chapel, District Six.

Muslim worshippers, District Six.

*2*

*3*

1 The 'Malay Quarter' on
  the slopes of Signal Hill.
2 Muslim home in the Bokaap.
3 District Six.

*C*ontrasts are a prominent feature of Cape Town, particularly in its architecture and culture. Some areas, such as Schotsche Kloof in the Malay Quarter and what remains of District Six, may appear somewhat dilapidated and insalubrious, but the buildings have an integrity and are part of a cohesive community, unlike the blight of the three apartment towers comprising the Disa Park complex on the far side of the city. Since their erection in the 1970s, they have offended the sensibilities of Capetonians and visitors alike – a visual degradation of an aspirant World Heritage Site. Tours to introduce visitors to the unique Cape Malay culture are conducted through Schotsche Kloof and its surrounds and can include a traditional meal incorporating the subtle spicy flavours of bobotie, breyani, smoorvis and a range of other tasty curries and snacks such as dhaltjies and samoosas. In reality, the Malay food of the Cape has more links with the cuisine of Indonesia than with that of Malaysia, but it is also influenced by the traditions of India, the Dutch and the French Huguenots.

Charming old homes in the Bokaap.
Al-Azhar – or Aspeling Street – Mosque, District Six.

Not all the early Indonesians at the Cape were slaves, for the colony was also used as a convict station and as a place of exile for high-ranking dissidents from the Dutch possessions in the East. The most famous of these was Sheikh Yusuf, a man of noble rank related to the kings of Goa and to one of the sultans of the Celebes. Much feared by the Dutch, he was sent into exile at the Cape at the age of 68. He died in 1699 and was buried some 20 kilometres from Cape Town. In the five years he spent here, Sheikh Yusuf gave enduring purpose and direction to the local Muslim community, and to this day his kramat, or tomb, is regarded as a holy place. Another leader who played a huge role in establishing Islam at the Cape was Tuan Guru. Of royal blood and an intellectual schooled in all aspects of the religion, he came to Africa in his middle age. He wrote prolifically and two of his most noted achievements during his sojourn

Kramat on Signal Hill, one of several around Cape Town.
Rose Street, Bokaap.

*here were his book on Islamic jurisprudence and his having written out the Qur'an from memory when he found that no copy existed here at the time. He also organised the first school for Cape Muslims in the Bokaap where he lived, died and is buried. Although the impact of the Islamic faith is largely contained within the Muslim community, the broader aspects of their Indonesian culture has had a considerable influence on life at the Cape. For instance, many Malayu words were absorbed into the Dutch spoken locally and today they are very much part of the Dutch-derived Afrikaans language. But it is in matters of food that the impact has been arguably the greatest, for the dishes and delicacies that were brought from the East have given rise to a unique culinary tradition known as Cape Malay.*

Preparing sweet-smelling sachets for the celebration of the Prophet's birthday is the prerogative of female members of the Muslim community.

*D*espite its fervent following of today, Islam – as one commentator has observed – did not come to the Cape as an already established way of life; instead it grew into one with time. The reason behind the statement is that for the most part the forebears of the Cape Malays were brought to this country in the seventeenth and eighteenth centuries as slaves, not from Malaysia as their name would suggest, but from the Indonesian Archipelago – islands such as Bali, Timor, Buton, Java and the Celebes – an area that had only just begun to absorb Islam. (Recent authorities state that significant numbers of Muslims were also brought to the Cape from India and other parts of Africa.) At the time that the slaves arrived – there were four main influxes from the 1660s through to the mid-1700s – the young colony was woefully short of skilled labour and it was an opportunity for the Indonesians to carve a niche for themselves. Although many came from rural backgrounds,

The traditions of the community are passed from one generation to the next.

*they quickly adapted to life in a town and soon formed a sophisticated community plying trades from carpentry and masonry through to tailoring and shoemaking. Some, on payment of a fee to their owners, were permitted to live and work independently. Such freedom enabled them to hold religious meetings in their homes and these, together with their common language of Malayu, kept the slaves in contact with one another, leading to a strong bond and the growth of a Muslim culture with attracted non-Muslims as well. The unifying devotion to the Islamic faith kept the community together during a period of some 150 years when public expression of any religion other than that of the Dutch was forbidden. But the focus of Muslim life is the mosque, and after the community had petitioned long and hard to build one, permission was finally granted in 1807. Today there are few areas in the Peninsula that are beyond earshot of a muezzin calling the faithful to prayer.*

The cable cars cross under the mountain's shadow.

The new revolving cable car.

The new restaurant on the mountain summit.

The upper cable station (above), and the interior of the mountain-top restaurant (below).

*I*t was not unusual for the cable-car service to the summit of Table Mountain to suffer periodic disruption owing to high winds or poor visibility, but in 1997 the journey, which for so long has been high on the 'must do' list for visitors to Cape Town, suffered the longest interruption in its 60-year history. This time, however, it was not a result of inclement weather, but because a new cable-way system was being installed. In late 1997, the service reopened to much fanfare. The new cable cars, which hold 65 passengers, makes the ascent, and descent, in only five minutes and, because of the new twin-cable system, have added stability so that the cars are able to operate even in fairly high winds. The cars also revolve to give passengers a 360-degree view of the mountain, city and bay on the way up and down. Facilities at the summit have also been redeveloped and include a restaurant and wine bar with breathtaking views from the sheer cliffs overlooking Camps Bay and the Atlantic seaboard. But for sheer romance on a balmy summer's evening, there is little to beat chosen company, a good bottle of wine and a picnic supper to be enjoyed away from the crowd while watching the sun go down on another glorious day.

1 From the top of Table Mountain, Cape Point lies on the distant horizon.
2 Viewing points above the sprawling city.
3 The Atlantic seaboard from the mountain peaks.
4 A quiet moment to admire the spectacle.
5 Rock hyraxes, or dassies.

4

5

*T*he cable way may provide easy access to the top of Table Mountain, but there is really only one way to explore this extraordinary mountain, soon to become recognized as a World Heritage Site, and that is by foot. The various faces of the mountain and the front and back table (seen here) are criss-crossed by hundreds of pathways, some of them no more difficult than an easy stroll, others more taxing and steep. Climbing routes, too, abound but these are not to be tried by the uninitiated and certainly never without the supervision of an experienced mountaineers. In fact, Table Mountain is never to be taken lightly as even the safest routes can become a nightmare when bright sunlight is obliterated in minutes by unpredictable clouds and mists that can come swirling over the crags and valleys. The golden rule is never to walk on Table Mountain alone, without adequate water and without warm clothing and a good map. Always let someone know your route, and stick to it, and best of all go in the company of someone who knows the mountain and its many moods. Dangers notwithstanding, Table Mountain is also a place of joy and tranquillity, where some 1 400 species of flowering plants are to be found – more than in any area of comparable size anywhere in the world.

Towards Mouille Point from the Sea Point Pavilion and, left, Sea Point with Table Mountain rising above the saddle between Signal Hill and Lion's Head.

O*n the other side of Signal Hill from the city and the Malay Quarter overlooking it, lies a very different Cape Town. Here, instead of the low, simple buildings in the styles of the past, tall apartment blocks line the coast in a manner more reminiscent of Rio de Janeiro and Hong Kong than the leisurely atmosphere usually associated with Cape Town. There is little of architectural merit in the untidy jostle for command of the best views over the ocean and some parts of the suburb, set back from the front rank, are*

*somewhat run-down. There is a vibrancy about the area, however, and at one time Sea Point was the undisputed epicentre of Cape Town nightlife. In its heyday, there were probably more restaurants here than in the rest of the city put together, but although a number remain and some are well patronized, Capetonians and visitors alike now have a choice of excellent venues spread throughout the city, the Waterfront development a few kilometres down the coast, and the suburbs.*

Originally restored by shipping magnate Sir John Ellerman in 1962, Ellerman House (above and right), the aristocratic villa in Bantry Bay, is an intimate, exclusive hotel favoured by Cape Town's ever-increasing procession of visiting notables.

*T*here is something about Clifton that suggests nouveau riche, *a glimpse into the 'lifestyles of the rich and famous'. And the sense of Mediterranean playground, that combination of highly developed mountainside, white beaches and sparkling sea, is even stronger in summer when the cars of beachgoers make narrow Victoria Road all but impassable, and motor cruisers and yachts crowd into Clifton Bay. For the most part, the homes and apartments that cling tenaciously to the steep slopes above the beaches are expensive, very expensive, and a number are owned by European émigrés who have bought their place in the sun at very favourable exchange rates. Most of the houses and apartments are new and adventurous, their contemporary designs a test of engineering skill and the determination of owners to achieve that perfect view. For many, the only access to their homes is via daunting flights of steps, but at least one homeowner has installed a funicular railway to provide an easy ride to his eyrie high on the flanks of Lion's Head.*

1  Clifton's sun-kissed beaches.
2  The white sands lining Clifton Bay.
3  A Clifton mansion, Victoria Road.

*Victoria Road, running southwards from Sea Point, climbs rapidly out of the high-rise tumble of hotels and apartment blocks to round the rocky headland of Bantry Bay. In doing so, it enters a very different world – if Sea Point is South Africa's Copacabana, then Clifton is its Cìte d'Azur. Here Lion's Head rises steeply to its summit 669 metres above the sea, while below the road that snakes its way around the lower slopes, the land drops almost precipitously to the Atlantic Ocean and the tiny crescents of white sand known rather prosaically as First, Second, Third and Fourth beaches. On a cold wintry day,*

*wrapped up warmly and enveloped in the thunder of heavy seas, the beaches are a place for solitude and a slow walk. In summer, however, Clifton Bay transforms into a mecca for sunworshippers. Undeterred by the surf that remains so cold throughout the year that it snatches your breath away, they flock to the beaches to watch and be watched as their tans deepen. One of the great advantages of Clifton, aside from its unparalleled setting, is that it is one of the few places protected by a quirk of geography from the Southeaster, that notorious summer wind that can nag at the Peninsula for days at a time.*

Camps Bay, above, is watched over by the Twelve Apostles. Bakoven, left, from the air.

*C*amps Bay is one of Cape Town's most beautiful suburbs. Less ostentatious than Clifton, perhaps, it is nevertheless a refuge of the city's moneyed citizens. Its setting is incomparable, with spacious homes and gardens below the soaring buttresses of the Twelve Apostles that together form the western face of the Table Mountain massif. Unfortunately, much of Camps Bay regularly feels the full brunt of the summer Southeaster, but this does little to detract from the popularity of the suburb or its long, wide beach. An undoubted focus of entertainment in Camps Bay is The Bay Hotel; stylish and sophisticated, it caters for overseas visitors and a growing executive clientele eager for an alternative to staying in the city centre. In the adjacent shopping mall is the rather noisy, but hugely popular, Blues Restaurant and its new neighbour

The Bay Hotel, Camps Bay.

*the Vilamoura. A little way down the palm-lined front is the ever-popular La Med a loud, boisterous watering hole and restaurant where, on a hot summer's evening, you could die of thirst in the struggle to win the attention of a barman. At Camps Bay's southern extremity is the much smaller Bakoven Bay, so-named for the low, rounded rock that bulges out of the surf just offshore. Clearly visible in the wall of the domed boulder is a smoothly curved opening, the overall effect being remarkably like that of a 'bakoven', the Dutch world for a clay baking oven. The tight little community of cottages that cluster around Bakoven Bay marks the boundary of suburbia and, for several kilometres, Victoria Road winds free of development, except for the eyesore of a half-completed hotel complex, towards the exclusive hamlet of Llandudno.*

*1*

*2    3*

*4*

1  Panoramic sweep of Clifton.
   and Camps Bay.
2  Llandudno.
3  Camps Bay.
4  Beachfront, Camps Bay.
5  Sunworshipping, Camps Bay.

*T*he Cape Peninsula has a coastline of nearly 150 kilometres and, for a good part of its length, the peaks of the Table Mountain chain fall steeply into the sea. Here and there, however, the cliffs give way to a stretch of brilliant white sand. A few of these beaches – Noordhoek and Muizenberg, for instance – curve lazily into the distance, while others such as the beaches of Clifton, Llandudno, Boulders and St James are little more than tucked-away coves. Some are great for bathing and some for the more adventurous sports of board-sailing and surfing, but all have their devotees and during Cape Town's long, hot, dry summer that extends from the end of October through to April – and sometimes even into May – many are invaded daily by those keen to soak up the sun.

The fishing village of Hout Bay.

Rural Hout Bay.

Kronendal Restaurant on Main Road.

*To early seafarers hugging the western flank of the Peninsula as they sailed to and from Table Bay, the deep haven a few sea miles down the coast – guarded by cliffs dropping sheer into the sea – must have soon become a familiar sight. It wasn't long before the bay was explored and its wooded valley noted with interest. Indeed, it was called* Houtbaai, *literally* Wood Bay, *and has retained this name to the present. We know that soon after his arrival, Jan van Riebeeck, first commander of the settlement, dispatched a party to investigate the bay and its surrounds, and it was not long after that that the exploitation of the bay for its timber began. As the*

*settlement at the foot of Table Mountain grew, so did the demand for timber. Soon the slopes of the mountain were cropped of their forest and resources farther afield, such as those at Hout Bay, were greedily attacked. It is probably only because the upper slopes of the valley were largely inaccessible that the forest survived to enjoy its present-day protected status. For much of the valley's history, timber and farming were the major sources of revenue. Today Hout Bay is a burgeoning town with tourism and fishing as the centre of its economic life. Indeed, the two activities go hand in hand, for the busy life in the harbour is a perennial attraction to visitors.*

1

The harbour with its fleet of brightly painted fishing smacks lies on the northern flank of Hout Bay, seemingly isolated from the bustle and frenetic energy of the city. Behind the fishing village tower the Sentinel and the Karbonkelberg to complete what must be one of the most photographed scenes in all of South Africa.

Quaint as it may appear, however, the harbour is a busy place, for it is the headquarters of the local crayfishing industry as well as other important fisheries. Synonymous with Hout Bay is snoek – a voracious predatory fish that is a highly regarded local delicacy – and during the season the incoming boats are eagerly met by those impatient to buy their evening meal fresh from the dockside.

2

3

With a history almost as old as that of Cape Town, Hout Bay is in a sense a microcosm of the city, sharing similar opportunities and problems. Cape Town bears the dubious honour of being one of the fastest-growing cities in the world, and certainly many of Hout Bay's residents feel that their share of the experience is rather discomforting. Yet the casual visitor may find this difficult to believe, for the bayside and adjacent valley have an idyllic quality, and this is enhanced by the undeniably spectacular setting. The village and lovely beach impart an air of permanent holiday, a laid-back atmosphere that is very seductive. Indeed, it is these qualities that have made Hout Bay a very desirable place in which to live.

1 Hout Bay from the fishing harbour.
2 Lunch in the fresh air of the seaside village.
3 The fishing boats of Hout Bay harbour.
4 Local fishermen haul in the snoek.
5 Dried fish is a popular Cape delicacy.

4

5

79

Chapman's Peak Drive, above and below, winds south over the peak from Hout Bay.

*T*he gradient of the coastal road as it leaves Hout Bay on its way towards Noordhoek is indeed impressive. It marks the start of Chapman's Peak Drive, a tortuous route that was literally carved out of the mountainside by convicts between 1916 and 1922. Rising and falling, twisting and turning, the road follows the fault line between the layer of granite, which drops away – in places some 200 metres – to the surging tides below, and the Table Mountain sandstone, which reaches the peaks of Constantiaberg, Noordhoek and Chapman's itself. The views back towards Hout Bay and of mountains and crashing seas are superb, and the drive is considered to be among the most scenic routes in the world. This is also an excellent spot for a lesson in the geology of the Peninsula. Essentially, three types of rock make up the Table Mountain range: shales, here and there showing through on the lower slopes as reddish clay soils; Cape granite, very obvious as the rounded grey boulders extending from the lower slopes of the mountain chain down to the shore; and Table Mountain sandstone, a sedimentary rock laid down over the shales and granite. Some 250 million years ago, huge buckling and uplifting of the sedimentary deposits gave rise to the mountains – and time, wind and water have slowly sculpted them into the shapes we see today.

1

2

3

1 Surfing the waves at Kommetjie.
2 Sunset over the water off Kommetjie.
3 Kommetjie is the heart the
  Peninsula's crayfishing spots.

*After the residential grandeur and obvious wealth of Clifton, Camps Bay, Llandudno and Hout Bay, it is something of a relief to reach the enclave of Kommetjie where, among the milkwoods, many of the original beach cottages date back to the turn of the present century. But even here, things are changing and Kommetjie is growing apace – new houses are springing up as the village rapidly becomes a suburb of Cape Town. For the moment at least, the quaint charm of Kommetjie remains, even when the wind is right for the 'Outer Kom' break which brings an instant army of surfers.*

*The waters of Kommetjie, and indeed the entire western coast of the Cape Peninsula, are without exception cold. Even in summer, not many swimmers are prepared to numb body and soul. But some of the best surfing and crayfishing spots are along this coast, and it is common to see wetsuited figures skimming down the face of a wave or bobbing about next to a fishing boat just behind the surf line.*

Noordhoek beach, with Kommetjie and the Slangkop lighthouse in the distance.

Seashore life of the Cape coast.

Chacma baboons.

*Noordhoek beach, that long stretch of uninterrupted white sand between the cliffs below Chapman's Peak Drive and far-off Kommetjie, is one of the loneliest spots on the entire Peninsula. Its inviting but treacherous waters make swimming inadvisable and the reputation of quicksand adds a sense of lurking danger, an almost primal quality, to the landscape. Early man lived in these parts, as we know from findings in nearby Peer's Cave – above Fish Hoek – that date back 25 000 years, and it is not difficult to imagine our Stone Age ancestors as part of the setting. Any such reverie is quickly dispelled, however, on casting one's eyes inland. The beach marks the western limit of the Noordhoek Valley which extends through to the town of Fish Hoek on the False Bay coast. Here the scene is very different from that which would have confronted Fish Hoek Man, for the valley, which incorporates valuable wetlands, is rapidly being transformed by suburban housing developments and informal settlements, while the indigenous vegetation is seriously threatened by invading alien plants.*

Smitswinkel Bay, from the Cape of Good Hope Nature Reserve.

Steenbok.

Bontebok.

Angulate tortoise.

The wreck of *Thomas T. Tucker*.

*T*he number of people visiting the Cape of Good Hope Nature Reserve, part of the designated Cape Peninsula National Park stretching from Table Mountain and across the rocky spine to Cape Point in the south, now nears the million mark a year. The reserve is a wonderfully wild place in which to ramble and it also happens to be one of the most important botanical conservation areas on the Peninsula. Few stop, however, to explore the wonder of the fynbos vegetation and the other inhabitants of the reserve, as they hasten across the windswept plateau, impatient to reach Cape Point and the legendary meeting place of the Atlantic and Indian oceans. Whether they do meet here or whether the honour belongs to Cape Agulhas to the east is academic, but there is no argument that this tumble of granite rocks marks the divide between the icy waters of the Peninsula's western coast and the comparatively warmer waters of False Bay on its eastern flank.

1 The lighthouse perched above the waves at Cape Point.
2 The Two Oceans Restaurant, tucked unobtrusively into the mountainside.
3 Cape Point's new funicular railway.

As with Table Mountain, the facilities at Cape Point have been completely redeveloped. The old buses that used to grind their way up the steep road to the turning point just below the old lighthouse have been replaced by a new funicular railway, while the previously absurdly inadequate curio shop and kiosk have given way to a new complex that includes the Two Oceans Restaurant set into the cliffs looking out over False Bay towards Cape Hangklip. Great care has been taken to make the buildings as visually unobtrusive as possible and the developers and conservation authorities are to be commended for their sensitivity. The restaurant itself is big and extremely busy but, despite this, manages good food and a reasonably fast and friendly service. For diners lucky enough to have secured a window table, a hasty meal is not a priority, however, for the view is breathtaking and must surely win for the restaurant a setting that rates as among the most spectacular anywhere in the world.

Boulders Beach.

*O*n the winding coastal road back along the False Bay coast from Cape Point, and before one reaches the historic naval port of Simon's Town, is a tiny beach called Boulders. Long known as one of the very few refuges from the summer Southeaster, the tiny cove has in recent years acquired a new and international significance, for it has become the breeding ground for a substantial colony of endangered jackass penguins. So popular has a visit to the site become that the well-being of the birds is threatened by camera-wielding tourists who sometimes form an almost impenetrable human wall between the birds and their nests as they return from foraging sorties out to sea. Aside from the attractions of the penguins at Boulders Beach and the obvious scenic beauty of the False Bay coastline, there is often another very special treat in store for those who take the trouble to scan the sea. During the months from March through to November each year, southern right whales come to the southern Cape coast to calve and to mate. It is not unusual at this time to suddenly become aware of the long, dark shape of a whale rolling lazily in the swell, to see a massive fluked tail flick through the air, or to catch sight of the telltale V-shaped spout, the only hints of the huge mammal below the surface.

The breeding colony of jackass penguins at Boulders, above, is a popular drawcard for visitors, below.

1

2

1 Simon's Town, headquarters
  of the South African fleet.
2 St George's Street, Simon's Town.
3 Just Nuisance, Jubilee Square.

*A* quiet stroll along St George's Street, the main road of Simon's Town, reveals a quaint little village where time appears to have stopped at the turn of the century. There are obvious reminders of the present, of course, but an active and largely successful historical and conservation movement among residents and others has done much to ensure the survival of Simon's Town's architectural heritage. Among the many buildings of note are Admiralty House, the Residency – which, after many years as magistrates' courts, has been restored to house the Simon's Town Museum – and the Martello Tower, built in 1796 and now the Naval Museum.

Both Simon's Town and the bay on which it stands take their name from Simon van der Stel, and enterprising administrator who came to the Cape in 1679 as commander, and later governor, of the small settlement. He surveyed the bay in 1687 and recommended that it be used as a winter anchorage, a refuge from the fierce northwesterly storms that were proving such a hazard to shipping in Table Bay. In 1814, Simon's Town became the South Atlantic base for the Royal Navy and remained as such until 1957, when it was handed over to the South African Navy. Of the copious stories that are associated with the town, few can be as endearing as that of Able Seaman Just Nuisance, the Great Dane which befriended sailors during the Second World War and was officially enlisted into the Royal Navy.

3

1 & 2 Kalk Bay harbour under siege from a gale-force Southeaster.

*1*

*2*

*To the first Portuguese explorers of the late fifteenth century, the southern tip of the African continent was the Cape of Storms and it was only later that it became known as the Cape of Good Hope. But, when the full might of a summer Southeaster or a winter Northwester unleashes itself on the Cape Coast, it is not hard to sympathize with* those early mariners in their puny sailing ships. Most coastal cities of the world are windy places – it is in the nature of an interface between land and sea – but Cape Town seems to have won particular notoriety. In the winter months, low-pressure systems move in off the southern oceans to strike the Peninsula as wave after wave of cold fronts bring rain, sometimes hard

The sea at Camps Bay flattened by an offshore Southeaster.

and driven and sometimes little more than a gentle drizzle. This westerly movement continues throughout the year, although in summer cooling in the northern hemisphere forces these systems further towards the Antarctic and they pass well to the south of the country. It is during these warmer months that the weather pattern is dominated by the strong South Atlantic high-pressure systems, bringing with it the mostly dry Southeaster. Along the western Cape coastline, where there is an abundance of rocky headlands and mountains rising close to the sea, the wind speed is increased. For instance, at Cape Point it may reach gale force almost every day during summer.

1 & 2 Kalk Bay harbour.

*O*n the False Bay coast, northwards from Simon's
Town through to Muizenberg, a number of ham-
lets, villages, and towns line the scenic rail route running
just above the high water mark. Of them, the adjacent
settlements of Kalk Bay, with its tiny fishing harbour,
and St James, with its postage-stamp beach lined with
gaily painted bathing booths, are the prettiest. St James is
also one of the few coves along this stretch of coast that
is protected from the Southeaster.

Bathing booths on the beach at St James.

*Kalk Bay derives its name from the Dutch word* kalk, *meaning lime, an allusion to the shells that were burnt to produce the main ingredient of the whitewash used for painting buildings. Fishing, however, has been the more enduring activity of Kalk Bay and the suitability of its natural harbour for this pursuit was noted as early as Simon van der Stel's explorations of the area in the late 1600s. As a result, it became an important whaling station, but this industry fell on hard times in the early years of the nineteenth century and, gradually, a more glamorous era began. The village was subsequently dubbed by a commentary in the Cape Monitor as a 'salubrious and fashionable watering hole – the Brighton of the Cape'.*

Muizenberg beach.

*Like Kalk Bay and St James, the suburb of Muizenberg, neatly arranged along the lower slopes of the mountain of the same name, was a fashionable seaside resort during the later years of Queen Victoria's reign and on into the early part of the new century. It was one of Rudyard Kipling's favourite places and his enthusiasm for the area and its beautiful, wide beach was shared by, among many others, Cecil John Rhodes. After the humiliating events leading up to the Anglo-Boer War, Rhodes retired to his home on the Main Road and died there soon afterwards. Rhodes' Cottage, as it is now known, is maintained as a museum and contains many of the extraordinary man's personal possessions. It is one of a number of buildings of historical and architectural importance in the village; others include the Posthuys which is believed to have been completed in 1673, a*

*year before the Cape Town castle, as well as Sandhills, Rust en Vrede and Vergenoeg (top right) which all bear the gracious stamp of Sir Herbert Baker's prolific genius. Muizenberg still shows some of its Victorian and Edwardian charm – on its quaint Victorian station, for example, stands the old clock tower (top left) – but, no longer in vogue, it now has an air of being simply 'old-fashioned'. In recent years, attempts have been made to inject new life into the area – the elaborate pavilion being an example – but essentially Muizenberg is a sleepy resort that wakens each year for just a few months of holiday activity, and then subsides once more into an extended winter hibernation.*

1  The Muizenberg stretch of the False Bay coast.
2  Muizenberg beach – the view towards St James.
3  Sunrise over Muizenberg beach.

*O*n a clear, still morning with the sun rising over the distant Hottentots Holland mountain range, Muizenberg beach forms an incomparable backdrop to False Bay. One of the safest and most popular bathing spots in all the Peninsula, its white sands slope gradually to the water's edge and continue eastwards as far as the eye can see; but for the rocky intrusion from far-off Wolfgat to Swartklip, they extend without interruption clear across False Bay to the towns of Strand and Gordon's Bay. False Bay derives its name from the fact that early navigators returning from the East often mistakenly assumed Cape Hangklip, the massive headland at the eastern limit of the bay, to be Cape Point. As they discovered, they had not rounded the Cape to enter Table Bay and hence the appellation, False Bay.

The front gable, Groot Constantia.
Groot Constantia.

*W*ine was made at the Cape not long after the Dutch first landed. It probably wasn't very good wine, but it was wine none the less – and so began a tradition of winemaking. In recent years particularly, Cape wines have made great strides in complexity and sophistication and have placed South Africa firmly on the map of the world's winemaking nations. As with so many aspects of Cape culture and early development, it was the colony's first governor, Simon van der Stel, who laid the foundation of the wine industry in South Africa. It was during his tenure that the town of Stellenbosch – considered to be the country's wine capital – was founded; it was he who settled French Huguenots in the Franschhoek Valley which is also a focus of winemaking; and it was he who saw the potential of the Constantia Valley. In this beautiful – and still remarkably rural –

Entrance to Klein Constantia.
The old wine cellar, Groot Constantia, now part of the museum.

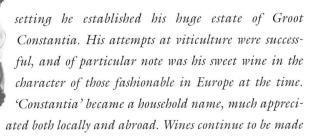

setting he established his huge estate of Groot Constantia. His attempts at viticulture were successful, and of particular note was his sweet wine in the character of those fashionable in Europe at the time. 'Constantia' became a household name, much appreciated both locally and abroad. Wines continue to be made in the Constantia Valley, and although greatly reduced from its original extent, Groot Constantia is still a working wine farm with a vast modern cellar. After a devastating fire in 1925, the stately homestead was faithfully restored to the faáade and additions made at the end of the eighteenth century. It is now a museum, while the outbuildings form a complex of restaurants, taverns and shops.

The homestead and vineyards of Buitenverwachting.

Constantia Valley landscape.

The old cellar, Buitenverwachting.

The wines of Groot Constantia are still well regarded but, during the 1980s and 1990s, winemaking in the valley has undergone something of a renaissance with the farms of Klein Constantia and Buitenverwachting, both owing their origins to Van der Stel's original estate, producing Chardonnays, Sauvignon Blancs and Bordeaux-style reds to match the best the country has to offer. Klein Constantia has even produced a 'Vin de Constance', an outstanding recreation of the wines that made Constantia so famous in the eighteenth and nineteenth centuries. Not to be outdone, Buitenverwachting (the name means 'beyond expectation') has combined good winemaking with good food and boasts one of the finest and most exclusive restaurants in South Africa. Food is also the focus at two other nearby venues – Constantia Uitsig and the restaurant/hotel complex of Steenberg Estate set amid the golf green.

1

2

1  Klein Constantia.
2  Riding in Constantia.
3  Wine tasting at Klein Constantia.

*For the people who live among the vineyards of the Constantia Valley or in any of the other adjacent suburbs, the mountain is literally their back garden and there is a sense of camaraderie among those taking their leisure on its slopes. It is a favourite place for wandering with a dog, riding along one of the many bridle paths, or testing one's fitness over an arduous jogging route. If the wealth of the homeowners along Cape Town's Atlantic seaboard manifests itself rather obviously, then the opposite is true in the southern suburbs that are ranged under the shadow of Table Mountain's eastern flank. In many parts – Constantia, Kenilworth, Bishopscourt, Wynberg Hill and Newlands, for example – the homes are no less opulent, but they stand discreetly behind tall hedges and at the end of long, treed driveways. Even where the homes are more modest, clustered in Wynberg's Little Chelsea or lining some of the suburbs' major streets, the lifestyle is rather less frenetic than it is in the Atlantic suburbs. Everywhere the forest-clad mountain looms as a backdrop, lending a sense of space which is enhanced by public parks and gardens.*

The library at Hawthornden.

*O*ff Herschel Walk – which, like the famous school on its lower reaches, takes its name from Sir John Herschel who did much to foster education in the colony – stands Hawthornden, one of the most admired Victorian/Edwardian residences in the southern suburbs. Set behind elegant cast-iron railings and amid a well-tended garden, the grand style of the present house – commissioned by one Captain John Spence and making its appearance in 1882 – was based on De Oude Wynberg, the original homestead built in 1775. Later the property was purchased by mining magnate Sir Joseph ('JB') Robinson who commissioned Sir Herbert Baker to refurbish the library, and made several other additions to the home. Now owned by Sir Joseph's grandson, Count

Tabora Manor House, Newlands.

*Natale Labia, the beautifully proportioned mansion boasts a renowned art collection (including a Van Dyck School portrait of Princess Mary, opposite). Many stately homes and historic buildings lie unassumingly and mostly hidden within the southern suburbs: Stellenberg in Kenilworth, with its magnificent homestead and outbuildings; cottages in Wynberg built in the* cottage orné *manner of Regency times; the large and sinister Jac Loopuyt House in Rondebosch, commonly referred to as the* spookhuis *(ghost house); and Tabora (above) in Newlands... all are part of the Cape's rich heritage. Not to be overlooked are the churches, particularly Herbert Baker's St Saviour's in Claremont, and even a few commercial buildings such as Josephine Mill, beautifully restored as a cultural centre where, with its again-turning waterwheel providing the power, flour is ground as it was in the early nineteenth century.*

*Fine wines, fine food, fine architecture and fine education would be a reasonable if not simplistic summation of Cape Town's cosmopolitan southern suburbs. The area has more than its fair share of sophisticated hotel complexes and shopping centres where wine shops, clothing boutiques, jewellers, cinemas, restaurants, and health shops rub shoulders along wide marbled pedestrian malls.*

*One of the more popular shopping centres in Cape Town is upmarket – and recently refurbished – Cavendish Square in Claremont, just a stone's throw away from Cape Town's mecca of sport, Newlands. The famous cricket and rugby stadiums have undergone major surgery in recent years to accommodate the demand for seats for the almost ceaseless programme of*

*international competitions played on their green fields. When 'big game fever' hits, even the limited parking facilities do little to deter the jostling, banner-waving enthusiasm of the occasion.*

*The suburbs around the Newlands sports complex are alive with hotels and guest houses, restaurants and pubs. Nearby is the lovely Vineyard Hotel with its beautifully landscaped gardens, while further afield are The Cellars-Hohenort and The Alphen, which retains the quiet elegance of its early history as the manor house of extensive vineyards. And when it comes to schools, such household names as Bishops, Herschel, Rondebosch Boys, SACS, Westerford, Wynberg and Rustenberg remain South Africa's oldest and most revered educational institutions.*

1 Alphen Hotel, Constantia.
2 The leafy avenues of Newlands.
3 Seat of learning for the boys of SACS.
4 Crowds pack the stands at Norwich Park.
5 Shoppers delight in the southern suburbs.
6 Bold, new Cavendish Square.

4

5

6

1 The University of Cape Town. 2 Groote Schuur. 3 'Physical Energy', Rhodes Memorial. 4 Jameson Steps, University of Cape Town.

*O*ne of Cape Town's grandest residences is Groote Schuur, another creation of Sir Herbert Baker, but not regarded among his best work. The history of the grand estate, however, predates Baker by some 250 years, for Groote Schuur's original structure was indeed the 'great barn' suggested by its Dutch name and was part of Jan van Riebeeck's granary. It was to pass through many owners before eventually coming into the hand of Cecil Rhodes, who commissioned the young Baker to create for him a mansion. After the fire which destroyed his original thatched restoration of Groote Schuur, Baker reconstructed the house with its familiar tall gables and 'barley sugar' chimneys.

Superlatives abound when one tries to do justice to the beauty of the Peninsula and the setting of its many famous landmarks, but even they are inadequate to describe the University of Cape Town, set into the slopes of Devil's Peak like some high monastic town. Like Groote Schuur it, too, owes its incomparable position to the vision of none other than Cecil John Rhodes whose spirit – his physical remains lie buried in the Matopo Hills of Zimbabwe – broods over his nearby memorial (left) which faces north towards the empire from Cape to Cairo that never materialized. The university has a highly respected medical faculty whose students train at the nearby Groote Schuur Hospital.

3

1

2

*S*prawling beneath the majestic buttress known as Castle Rock is Kirstenbosch, the loveliest public garden of all and, indeed, one of the greatest in the world. Only southern African plants are represented in the garden, making its extensive collection unique. The focus, however, is on the Cape flora which, although covering only four per cent of South Africa's land surface, comprises about 8 500 species and constituting one of the six floral kingdoms of the world.

4          5          6          7    8

*3*

1 Summertime concert, Kirstenbosch.
2 Path to Skeleton Gorge.
3 Camphor tree avenue.
4 Featherheads.
5 Silver tree.
6 Agapanthus.
7 'Blou suikerbos' protea.
8 Erica.
9 River lily.
10 Pincushion.
11 Red disa.
12 Suurkanol.
13 Gousblom.
14 Bitter aloe.
15 Sunshine protea.

*A relatively new tradition of the gradens is Sunday evening concerts. Although some purists find fault with the gardens being subjected to such commercialism, most recognize the need for Kirstenbosch to secure its future through fund-raising efforts. The Sunday concerts serve such an end and have found great favour amongst the many who flock to the gardens, picnic hampers in hand, to enjoy a programme that might include anything from Mozart to traditional African music and jazz.*

9   10   11   12   13   14   15

Glass conservatory, Kirstenbosch.

*T*he Kirstenbosch gardens are much loved by Capetonians and are on the itinerary of anyone passing through the city. More than 600 000 visitors pass through every year, but even before the gates open at eight o'clock, regulars may sneak in through a side entrance to enjoy the peace and solitude of an early morning jog or amble in the gardens.

Even at weekends and on public holidays, Kirstenbosch never seems crowded, and a short walk beyond the well-beaten circuit around the

Castle Rock, Kirstenbosch.

upper restaurant and shop will always be rewarded with a sense of having the place to oneself. Not only does the network of paths lead one through the proteas, ericas, cycads, pelargoniums and other indigenous plants, but it also provides access to the mountain and two of the most popular ascents, up Nursery Ravine and Skeleton Gorge. One of the most recent innovations at Kirstenbosch is the massive Glass House with its fine collection of succulent flora, including a sizeable baobab.

1

*T*he front face of Table Mountain is bare and formidable, a continuous grey wall reaching to the apparently flat summit that gives the mountain its name. There are easy ascents such as the long slog up Platteklip Gorge, but many more are a testing challenge of the rock-climber's skills. But the mountain's eastern face is very different, deeply incised by steep, heavily wooded gorges which shelter delicate plants such as the red disa (opposite, bottom left). Lower down, the gorges spread out into sizeable areas of forest which turn this side of the mountain into a 'green and pleasant place' of shaded pathways and waterfalls. Of the many mountain walks on the eastern flank of the mountain, one of the most enjoyable is to take a stroll along the contour path that is easily accessed from Constantia Nek, Kirstenbosch and other points. Once on the contour path proper, the going is generally easy and the hike through the forests, with glimpses now and again of the sprawling suburbs below, is most enjoyable, even on a hot summer's day.

1 Skeleton Gorge on the eastern
face of Table Mountain.
2 Pine plantation in Cecelia
State Forest.

2

*From the wetland reserve of Rietvlei on the west coast north of Table Bay, the
view of Table Mountain and its companions, Lion's Head and Devil's Peak, is
probably little different from that gazed upon by human beings thousands upon thousands of
years ago. It is not hard, especially when a low mist hangs over the sea, to imagine that there is no
city there at all and, like the first European explorers who approached from the north in their tiny
sailing ships, that the land on the distant horizon is simply an island rising out of the sea...
But there is a difference. Gone are the people who gathered food from the sea and grazed their
cattle on the plains, gone are the hippos that snorted in the Liesbeek River and the lions that
once hunted in Table Valley, and gone is much of the natural vegetation that evolved in
concert with the climate, geology and animal life. The environment of the Cape Peninsula
has been irrevocably altered by the hand of man, and in times of reflection it is difficult
not to feel guilt at our presumption. On the other hand, our interference has created
Cape Town, one of the most beautiful and exciting cities in all the world.*